British Railway Picto

Scottish Region 1948-67

Brian J. Dickson

Ian Allan
PUBLISHING

CONTENTS

This book is dedicated to the memory of Cyril Avery

First published 2006

ISBN (10) 0 7110 3176 2
ISBN (13) 978 0 7110 3176 0

© Brian J. Dickson 2006

Published by Ian Allan Publishing

an imprint of Ian Allan Publishing Ltd,
Hersham, Surrey KT12 4RG
Printed in England by Ian Allan Printing Ltd,
Hersham, Surrey KT12 4RG

Code: 0607/B2

Visit the Ian Allan Publishing website at
www.ianallanpublishing.com

Front cover:
On a beautiful summer's day in August 1954
ex-GNSR Class V (LNER Class D40) 4-4-0
No 62262 leaves Craigellachie with a goods
for Aviemore. Built in 1899, this locomotive
would survive a further year before
withdrawal in late 1955. *Eric Russell /
Colour-Rail SC165*

Back cover (top): The yard at Killin station
during the summer of 1959. Looking well
cared for, the locomotive, built at St Rollox
Works in 1914, would be withdrawn in 1961.
P. J. Hughes / Colour-Rail SC749

Back cover (middle):
Ex-LNER Class K4 2-6-0 No 61995 *Cameron
of Lochiel* takes water at Crianlarich Upper
whilst operating a special on the West
Highland line from Fort William to Glasgow
in June 1960. *F. Hornsby / Colour-Rail SC79*

Back cover (bottom):
A relative stranger to the north of Scotland,
English Electric Type 4 diesel-electric
No D252, heads a down goods through
Dingwall in July 1967. *Eric Doel*

Left:
Leaving the gloom beneath the cavernous
overall roof at Edinburgh's Princes Street
station, ex-LMS Class 5MT 4-6-0 No 45161
bursts into bright sunlight as it heads a local
stopper to Glasgow Central via Shotts on
8 July 1952. *Sidney E. Teasdale*

Title page:
A classic scene at the eastern end of Waverley
station in Edinburgh in the summer of 1961,
with ex-LNER Class A4 Pacific No 60009
Union of South Africa departing with the up
'Elizabethan' bound for King's Cross non-stop.
In the background 'Peak' Type 4 No D11,
sporting a Leeds Neville Hill shedplate, waits
to leave with a train for St Pancras via the
Waverley route to Carlisle and thence over
the Settle & Carlisle to Leeds. *Eric Treacy*

INTRODUCTION

The period from January 1948 until June 1967, not quite 20 years in duration, saw some of the greatest changes to the railways in Scotland. Nationalisation brought a feeling of renewal within the management of the railways, especially after the dark days of World War 2, when prewar standards of maintenance had been difficult to maintain. New, powerful modern locomotives were starting to appear, LNER-designed types such as the Class K1 Moguls and Class A1 Pacifics being built and delivered throughout 1948, 1949 and 1950, while Class B1 4-6-0s continued to be delivered until 1952. Mixed-traffic locomotives based upon LMS designs also continued to appear, Ivatt-designed Class 2MT 2-6-0s and 2-6-2 tanks remaining in production until 1953. The last examples of the Stanier 'Black Five' 4-6-0, which first appeared in 1934, were still being delivered during 1951.

The appearance in Scotland of the BR Standard classes from 1951 brought improved working conditions for the footplate crews, but there was no real improvement to the poor state of some locomotive depots. Many depots had gaping holes in their roofs, and poor working and lighting conditions prevailed for the staff undertaking the maintenance of locomotives. Many coaling plants at depots still relied on manual labour to fill tubs prior to coaling locomotives, and (to take one example) coaling at St Margarets

depot in Edinburgh continued to be handled in this way until its closure in 1967.

In the 1950s, as larger sums of money were allocated to the railways, track maintenance and quality improved, allowing higher running speeds. In Scotland this culminated in what is regarded as the highlight of steam-locomotive operation during the 1960s, with the reintroduction in 1962 of the three-hour fast expresses between Glasgow and Aberdeen using ex-LNER Class A4 Pacifics. Ten of these locomotives were transferred to Ferryhill depot in Aberdeen and St Rollox depot in Glasgow to operate these services, which they did successfully until the summer of 1966, when the five Aberdeen-based survivors were withdrawn.

The operation of diesel multiple-units (DMUs) began in Scotland with the introduction in January 1957 of Swindon-built 'Inter-City' units on services between Edinburgh (Waverley) and Glasgow (Queen Street). The use of DMUs quickly spread to other passenger routes as more units became available, and this, together with the closure of many branch lines to passenger traffic during the 1950s, meant that large numbers of steam locomotives were disposed of.

Main-line diesel locomotives started to appear in Scotland during 1959, initially being allocated to depots in the north of Scotland, and as more became available they displaced all steam motive power on traffic north of Perth and Aberdeen. This was achieved by the summer of 1961, by which time diesel locomotives had also replaced steam on Glasgow–Fort William–Mallaig and Glasgow–Oban

services. This resulted in large numbers of steam locomotives being transferred south or sent to scrapyards.

November 1960 saw Scotland's most ambitious railway-modernisation project come to fruition with the launch of Glasgow's 'Blue Train' electric services, and once technical problems, which brought about their temporary withdrawal shortly after their introduction, had been resolved these proved enormously popular with the travelling public.

By the mid-1960s steam locomotives were rapidly disappearing from Scotland as larger numbers of reliable diesel locomotives were allocated to Scottish depots. Coal trains from the Ayrshire coalfields became diesel-hauled in 1966, and the last few BR steam locomotives in Scotland finished their days shunting in colliery yards in the West Lothian and Fife coalfields, the last two examples being officially withdrawn in June 1967.

Acknowledgements
Thanks are due to Peter Waller at Ian Allan Publishing for granting access to the company's extensive photographic archive; also to the hard-working editors, designers and production staff who have had to manage the progress of this book. Thanks are also due to Brian Lewis and Reg Carter of the Stephenson Locomotive Society, for their assistance with fact-finding and access to the photographic material in their archive. Special thanks go to Allan Vigar, for information on locomotive No 1649, and to the Glasgow & South Western Railway Association, for details relating to route indicators.

Right:
A busy scene at the western end of Waverley station in Edinburgh on 4 August 1959, witnessed by a couple of young enthusiasts. Standard Class 4MT 2-6-0 No 76102 manœuvres light-engine while an unidentified 0-6-0 diesel-electric shunter, acting as one of the station pilots, shunts some empty stock. In the background are two Class A3 Pacifics.
R. M. Hay

1. JANUARY 1948 TO DECEMBER 1950

From Nationalisation to the eve of the introduction of the BR Standard steam locomotives

January 1948 dawned brightly for the new 'British Railways', run by the Railway Executive for the British Transport Commission. Its main objective was to restore the railway service to prewar standards. It became the owner of a large number of locomotives, the majority of which were pre-Grouping classes badly in need of replacement with modern types. In Scotland this legacy consisted of more than 1,400 locomotives whose parentage was Caledonian Railway, Great North of Scotland Railway, Highland Railway or North British Railway; no Glasgow & South Western Railway locomotives survived into British Railways ownership. The majority — more than 1,300 — were of CR or NBR origin, and of these more than two thirds were of the 0-6-0 tender type.

During the post-Grouping period both the LMS and LNER had been replacing the older classes of locomotives with modern, more powerful examples from some English-based classes. One well-documented example was the transfer during the early 1930s of a number of ex-Great Eastern railway Class S69 (LNER Class B12) 4-6-0 locomotives to the ex-GNSR lines. These became the mainstay of services on the main-line sections, only to be replaced themselves during the early 1950s by Class B1 4-6-0 and Standard Class 4 2-6-0 locomotives. Another well-known example was the replacement of many ex-NBR locomotives — particularly the ageing Class D34 'Glen' 4-4-0s on the West Highland line from Glasgow to Fort William and Mallaig — by LNER Class K2 Moguls, many of which from 1925 were allocated to Eastfield depot in Glasgow and to Fort William to work this exacting route. They did so very successfully for many years, and it was not until after the end of World War 2 that a start was made in replacing them with new Class B1 4-6-0s.

Early in 1948 Mr R. A. Riddles, responsible for mechanical and electrical engineering, organised a committee to make recommendations concerning the standardisation of locomotive parts and the selection of the best of existing locomotive types that would form the basis for a future construction programme. The main criteria for new locomotives were that they should be cheap to build, economical to work, easy to service and repair, offer improved driving and firing conditions for crews and have a route availability that would enable them to work virtually anywhere on the system. The result was a list of 12 types ranging initially from a Class 7 Pacific to a Class 2 2-6-2 tank engine, with provision later for a heavy freight locomotive. All 12 types were to be built with two cylinders fitted with Walschaerts valvegear, self-cleaning smokeboxes, rocking grates and self-emptying ashpans.

During this period Scottish enthusiasts had to cope with several locomotive-numbering systems: first, that of the old LMS and LNER companies; second, the short-lived attempt by British Railways to prefix locomotive numbers with 'M' for Midland and 'E' for Eastern origin; and third, the final, more logical numbering sequence adopted by British Railways. A number of the photographs in this section illustrate this mixture of numbering styles, which prevailed for a couple of years while locomotives awaited a visit to the works for repair/overhaul, repainting and renumbering.

Below left:

Wednesday 21 April 1948

One of the oldest classes of ex-NBR locomotive to survive into British Railways ownership was the '18-inch Goods' Class C 0-6-0. These handsome-looking locomotives were classified 'J36' by the LNER and numbered over 160 examples, of which almost 120 survived to see service with British Railways. Designed by Matthew Holmes and introduced in 1888, they were progressively rebuilt by W. P. Reid during the early part of the 20th century, the most prominent modification being the larger cab. This photograph shows No 5243, not yet fitted with a vacuum brake, at Haymarket depot in Edinburgh. The tender still bears the abbreviated 'N E' initials, while the coal therein appears to be of very poor quality. Built in 1891, this locomotive was to serve for 75 years, not being withdrawn until 1966, and is now preserved on the Bo'ness & Kinneil Railway. *E. R. Wethersett*

Above right:

Thursday 22 April 1948

Built for the Great North of Scotland Railway by Manning Wardle & Co were four diminutive 0-4-2 tanks used specifically for shunting the lines in and around Aberdeen harbour. The first two locomotives, Class Y (LNER Class Z5), were delivered early in 1915; the second pair, Class X (LNER Z4), were slightly lighter and were delivered later in the year. One example of each class survived until 1960; pictured at Kittybrewster depot, Class Z4 No 8191, looking smart with its 'NE' inscription, would be withdrawn in 1959. *E. R. Wethersett*

Below:

Saturday 19 June 1948

This photograph illustrates the situation prevailing during the first year of Nationalisation, with many locomotives having to wait for entry into the workshops before they could don their new identities. Photographed at St Margarets depot in Edinburgh, ex-NBR Class G (LNER Class Y9) 0-4-0ST No 8092 (left) still retains its LNER identity, while sister locomotive No 68097 (right) gleams in its new British Railways livery. Built for shunting duties in docks and small sidings, examples of this class could be seen working in Edinburgh, Leith Docks, Dundee and Dunfermline. Built in 1882, No 8092 would be withdrawn (as 68092) in 1953 after 71 years of service; No 68097, built in 1887, would survive until 1958, having served the same number of years. Another of this class, No 68095, is preserved as a static exhibit by the SRPS at Bo'ness. *A. C. J. Ball*

Above:
Saturday 19 June 1948
Resplendent in garter blue, ex-LNER Class A4 Pacific No 60012
Commonwealth of Australia simmers quietly at Haymarket depot in
Edinburgh, having been prepared for its next duty. Built at Doncaster
Works in 1937, this locomotive would be allocated to Haymarket for
virtually its entire working life, moving to Aberdeen Ferryhill only in
the early 1960s to work the fast three-hour services between Glasgow
and Aberdeen. Withdrawal was to follow in 1964. *A. C. J. Ball*

Below:
Saturday 19 June 1948
The ex-LNER Class D11/2 4-4-0s were a post-Grouping development
of the 'Large Director' class designed by Robinson for the Great Central
Railway and introduced in 1920. Built specifically to the North British
loading gauge, they worked on the fast inter-city expresses between
Edinburgh and Glasgow and services to Fife and Dundee. Seen at
Haymarket depot in Edinburgh, No 62671 *Bailie MacWheeble* had been
built by Kitson & Co in 1924 and would be withdrawn from service
in 1961. *A. C. J. Ball*

Right:

Tuesday 22 June 1948
The photographer noted that his journey from Mallaig to Fort William on this day was by the 1pm service, which consisted of four corridor coaches and six fish vans. The locomotive used was ex-GNR Class H3 (LNER Class K2) 2-6-0 No 1789 *Loch Laidon*, which was painted in green livery and based at Mallaig depot. Built by Kitson & Co in 1921, it was to spend its entire working life in Scotland, ultimately being withdrawn in 1959. Here we see the locomotive at Mallaig prior to the journey. *A. C. J. Ball*

Below:

Wednesday 23 June 1948
Designed by W. P. Reid for the North British Railway and introduced in 1913, the 'Glen' (LNER Class D34) 4-4-0s were primarily intended to work the West Highland line to Fort William and its extension to Mallaig. The majority of these powerful, superheated locomotives were thus based at Eastfield depot in Glasgow, although smaller allocations could be found in Edinburgh and Fife. This photograph shows 1913-built No 2469 *Glen Douglas*, still in LNER livery, waiting at Alloa station at the head of a passenger train. In 1959 this locomotive would be restored to NBR livery, reverting to its NBR number (256) and being used on special workings until 1965. Retired to the Glasgow Transport Museum in 1965, it is currently on display at the SRPS museum at Bo'ness. *A. C. J. Ball*

Above:

Wednesday 23 June 1948

Although the NBR 'Superheated Scott' (LNER Class D30) was introduced in 1912, a year before the 'Glens', the two classes were being built contemporaneously throughout the years 1913-20, when the last examples of each left Cowlairs Works. The 'Superheated Scotts' were used on express passenger trains throughout the NBR system but could most commonly be found on the Waverley route between Edinburgh and Carlisle. Here, however, we see No 2441 *Black Duncan* at Stirling depot. Built in 1920, this locomotive would be withdrawn in 1958. The last two members of the class would survive until 1960. *A. C. J. Ball*

Left:

Wednesday 23 June 1948

Standing quietly at Stirling depot is ex-NBR Class B (LNER Class J37) 0-6-0 No 4544. Yet to be renumbered 64544, it bears all the pre-Nationalisation identity marks. The front buffer-beam shows its number, class and depot allocation — Stirling. The 'B' class were the unsuperheated sisters of the superheated 'S' class, identical in appearance, both types having been designed by W. P. Reid and introduced in 1914. Classified 'J37' by the LNER, they were rated as '5F' under BR's LMS-derived classification system. This locomotive, built in 1915, was to survive until 1962. *A. C. J. Ball*

Right:

Thursday 24 June 1948

In grimy workmanlike condition and still bearing its LMS identity, 'Small Ben' 4-4-0 No 14409 *Ben Alisky* stands outside Helmsdale depot. Built by the Highland Railway at its Lochgorm Works at Inverness in 1900 to a design introduced by Peter Drummond in 1898, this locomotive was one of a class of 20 built primarily for secondary passenger duties. By the time of its withdrawal in 1950 it would be one of only five examples still working. Regrettably the last survivor, No 54398 *Ben Alder*, withdrawn in 1953 and stored until 1967 with a view to preservation, was ultimately sent for scrap and not saved as a fine example of Highland Railway locomotive design. *A. C. J. Ball*

Above:

Thursday 24 June 1948

Photographed at Forres depot, ex-HR 'Loch' 4-4-0 No 14385 *Loch Tay* was the last survivor of a class of 18 locomotives designed by David Jones and built by Dubs & Co in 1896, primarily for express passenger duties on the Highland main line between Perth and Inverness. Displaced by the larger Highland 4-6-0 designs, they were later relegated to secondary duties. This locomotive would be withdrawn from service at Forres in 1950. *A. C. J. Ball*

Above:
Thursday 24 June 1948
Looking splendid in green livery and obviously well cared-for by its home depot of Keith, ex-GER Class S69 (LNER Class B12) 4-6-0 No 61503 quietly awaits its next duty at Elgin. Built in 1912 at Stratford Works, this locomotive and four other 'B12s' were transferred in 1931 within the LNER to Scotland, to work the GNSR section. As the decade progressed they were followed by many others, allocated to either Keith or Kittybrewster. This example would be withdrawn from service in 1951. *A. C. J. Ball*

Left:
Friday 25 June 1948
It is generally accepted that the Great North of Scotland Railway built some of the most graceful 4-4-0 locomotives ever to work in Great Britain. Lending credence to that view is this photograph of Class V No 2262 taken at Keith depot, showing the graceful curve of the splashers, the slender, slightly tapering chimney and the tall dome of this William Pickersgill design of 1899; classified 'D40' by the LNER, the locomotive still proudly wears that company's identity. Built by Neilson, Reid & Co in 1899, it would remain in service until 1955. *A. C. J. Ball*

Above:
Friday 25 June 1948
In a desolate scene at Inverurie Works scrapyard, ex-NBR Class M (LNER Class D31) 4-4-0 No 2069 is being reduced to scrap, its tender having already been stripped to the frames. Withdrawn from service late in 1947, this locomotive had been built in 1898 to a Matthew Holmes design introduced in 1884. In a similar state of destruction in the background is ex-GER Class S69 (LNER Class B12) 4-6-0 No 1531; built at Stratford Works in 1914 and transferred to the GNSR section in 1933, this locomotive was also withdrawn from service late in 1947. *A. C. J. Ball*

Right:
Friday 25 June 1948
Built in 1911 at Stratford Works, the first of the Holden-designed Class S69 4-6-0s for the GER (LNER Class B12) was transferred to the GNSR section at Keith depot in 1932. A grimy-looking No 1500 is seen awaiting its fate at Inverurie Works in the month of its withdrawal. *A. C. J. Ball*

Above:
Wednesday 14 July 1948
Considered by many as Sir William Stanier's masterpiece, the 'Princess Coronation' class formed the backbone of the motive power for express passenger services on the West Coast main line between London and Glasgow. Still bearing its LMS identity, No 6248 *City of Leeds* is seen departing Perth with an up express. Turned out by Crewe in 1943 as one of a batch of four fitted with streamlined casing, it would survive until 1964. *O. O. B. Herbert*

Left:
July 1948
Still bearing its LNER identity, ex-NBR Class L (LNER Class C16) 4-4-2 tank No 7500 approaches Blanefield station with an Aberfoyle–Glasgow service. The 'L' class was the superheated version of the earlier Class M (LNER Class C15) tank and was introduced in 1915 primarily for suburban work around Edinburgh and Glasgow. This example was built by the North British Locomotive Co in 1921 and would be withdrawn in 1959. *P. M. Alexander*

Above:

Monday 27 September 1948

Ex-HR 'Clan' 4-6-0 No 54767 *Clan Mackinnon* prepares to leave Kyle of Lochalsh station with a train of cattle wagons. Built in 1921 by Hawthorn Leslie to a design introduced in 1919, it was by now the last survivor of the class of eight; the only example to pass into British Railways ownership, it would be withdrawn from service early in 1950. *O. O. B. Herbert*

Right:

Wednesday 29 September 1948

One of the few surviving CR-designed 4-6-0s to pass to British Railways was Class 60 No 54639. Bearing its British Railways identity, it is seen working an up goods near Ninewells Junction, Dundee, on the ex-Caledonian route to Perth. Built by the LMS at St Rollox in 1926, it would be withdrawn from service in 1953, the last of the class to survive. *Gavin L. Wilson*

Above:

Monday 18 April 1949
Bearing no sign of ownership, ex-LMS Class 4MT 2-6-4 tank No 2190 waits at Greenock (Princes Pier) with a passenger train to Glasgow.
This was a Fairburn version of a design introduced by Fowler in 1927 and perpetuated throughout the 1930s and '40s and into the 1950s by
Stanier and Fairburn. In all, almost 600 examples were constructed, serving all over the LMS system. At the time of the photograph this example
was virtually brand-new, having been built at Derby in 1948; it would be withdrawn from service as No 42190 in 1964. *J. F. Henton*

Above:

Thursday 16 June 1949
Swinging on to the Deeside line at Ferryhill Junction, ex-GNSR Class F (LNER Class D40) 4-4-0 No 62276 *Andrew Bain* looks very smart bearing
its new British Railways livery at the head of a Ballater train. These graceful locomotives were designed by Thomas Heywood and numbered only
eight in total; this example was built by NBL in 1920 and would be withdrawn from service in 1955. *H. C. Casserley*

Above:

Saturday 18 June 1949

Seen at Dumfries is ex-CR Class 439 0-4-4T No 55164, one of the handsome 'Standard Passenger' tank engines, the design of which dated from the mid-1890s. More than 130 were constructed between 1895 and 1922, while a further 10 were built for the LMS in 1925. Variations were many: early examples were fitted with condensing gear, some later locomotives had larger water tanks and reinforced buffer-beams, while many would suffer the ignominy of having their handsome chimneys replaced by the stovepipe variety. In BR days they could still be seen working many of the ex-CR branch lines, notably those serving Killin, Moffat and Ballachulish. Built in 1900, this locomotive would remain in service until 1959. *A. C. J. Ball*

Right:

Saturday 18 June 1949

The ex-LMS Class 5 2-6-0s known as 'Horwich Crabs' were introduced in 1926 and designed as general-purpose locomotives. They were conceived during George Hughes' tenure at the old Lancashire & Yorkshire Railway works at Horwich, and although most were constructed there, some were built at Crewe. Seen at Stranraer depot, No 42908 was a Crewe example built in 1930 and would survive until 1966. *A. C. J. Ball*

Above:
Saturday 18 June 1949
One of several types of 0-6-0 produced by the CR was the McIntosh '812' class. Introduced in 1899, these sturdy locomotives were used on both passenger and goods trains. More than 70 were built, the majority surviving into BR days and not being withdrawn until the early 1960s. Seen at Ayr depot, No 57614 has been renumbered by BR, although the tender, not unusually for this period, still bears LMS lettering. One of the non-vacuum-braked examples built in 1900, this locomotive would be withdrawn in 1962 after 62 years of service. *A. C. J. Ball*

Below:
Saturday 18 June 1949
With superheated boilers, the NBR Class S 0-6-0s, designed by W. P. Reid, were intended specifically for working heavy goods — particularly Fife coal trains — and numbered more than 100 examples, built between 1914 and 1921. Classified as 'J37s' by the LNER, these powerful locomotives were eventually given a '5F' rating by British Railways, virtually all surviving until the early 1960s. This photograph, taken at Ayr depot, shows No 64605, built in 1919 and destined to be withdrawn from service in 1964. *A. C. J. Ball*

Right:
Saturday 18 June 1949
One of only two examples built, ex-LNER
Class V4 2-6-2 No 61701 is seen at Ayr depot.
Designed by Sir Nigel Gresley, the pair were
constructed in 1941 as a lighter version of the
'V2', allowing a wider route availability.
Both locomotives were allocated to Eastfield
depot in Glasgow and worked from there
until withdrawal in 1957 after a working life
of only 16 years. Originally numbered 3402
by the LNER, it became 61701 under BR
and was known unofficially as 'Bantam Hen';
classmate No 61700 bore the name
Bantam Cock. A. C. J. Ball

Above:
Sunday 19 June 1949
The North British Railway built more than 100 examples of its Class A 0-6-2 tank, designed by W. P. Reid and introduced in 1909 (and later
designated Classes N14 and N15 by the LNER). Seen at Eastfield depot in Glasgow is No 9131, still with Westinghouse brake equipment and also
fitted with slip-coupling gear to enable it to bank passenger trains out of Queen Street station. Built by NBL in 1910 and numbered 282 by the
NBR, it became LNER No 9282 following the Grouping and adopted 9131 in the 1946 renumbering; it would be withdrawn from service as BR
No 69131 in 1962. *A. C. J. Ball*

Above:
Sunday 19 June 1949
Intended primarily for shunting and short-distance goods trains, the Matthew Holmes-designed NBR Class D (LNER Class J83) 0-6-0 tanks were handsome locomotives. This view features No 68447 at Eastfield depot in Glasgow; built in 1900 by Neilson Reid & Co and originally numbered 800, it became LNER No 9800 after the Grouping and then 8447 in 1946. It would be withdrawn from service in 1961. *A. C. J. Ball*

Above:
Sunday 19 June 1949
Standing at Eastfield depot in Glasgow, ex-NBR Class B (LNER Class J35) 0-6-0 No 64504 appears to be out of steam awaiting attention. Introduced by the NBR with unsuperheated boilers in 1906, the 76 locomotives of this class were built to a design by W. P. Reid for general goods work. Most survived into British Railways ownership; built in 1910, this example would last until 1960. *A. C. J. Ball*

Above:

Sunday 19 June 1949

Introduced from 1912, the 23 0-6-0 tank engines of the CR's '498' class were officially designated 'Dock Tanks' but could be found shunting in goods yards in the Glasgow and Edinburgh areas. Classified '2F' by British Railways, No 56158 sports its new identity at Yoker depot in Glasgow. Built in 1915, it was to put in a total of 46 years' service, not being withdrawn until 1961. *A. C. J. Balll*

Above:

Sunday 19 June 1949

The ex-CR Class 782 0-6-0 tanks were larger in all respects than the '498s'. Later classified '3F' by British Railways, they were intended primarily for general shunting and short-trip goods work. Construction commenced in 1895. Together with the similar '29' class they numbered 147 examples and could be seen working in yards over most of the old Caledonian system. Here we see No 56339 looking smart in its new BR livery at Yoker depot in Glasgow; built in 1911, it would be withdrawn in 1956. *A. C. J. Ball*

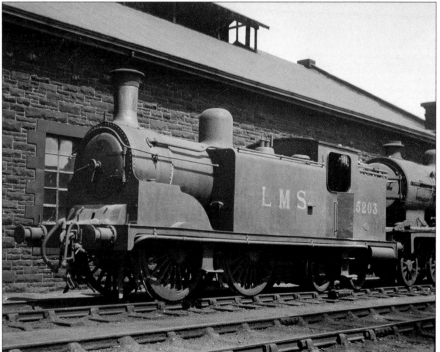

Above:
Sunday 19 June 1949
The Caledonian Railway's '264' class of
0-4-0ST locomotives was introduced in 1885
by Dugald Drummond and continued to be
built as required throughout the McIntosh
period. As small shunting locomotives they
could be found working into private sidings,
docks and small yards throughout the old
Caledonian system. Pictured at Motherwell
still bearing its LMS identity is No 16029,
built in 1895; seen attached to a wooden
'Engine Tender' and still bearing an LMS
28A (Motherwell) shedplate, it would remain
in service until 1962. In the background
is ex-CR '439' 0-4-4 tank No 15188.
A. C. J. Ball

Left:
Monday 20 June 1949
Still bearing its LMS identity, ex-CR
Class 439 0-4-4 tank No 15203 shows off
its handsome, sturdy lines while off-duty at
Hurlford depot. Built in 1910, this locomotive
spent almost its entire working life based at
Hurlford, where it would stay until withdrawal
in 1961. *A. C. J. Ball*

Above:

Monday 20 June 1949

Looking resplendent in its new black BR
livery, ex-CR Class 139 4-4-0 No 54452
rests between duties at Hurlford depot.
Built from 1907 to 1914, the 22 locomotives
of this class represented the culmination of the
'Dunalastair' series. Used initially on express
passenger trains throughout the Caledonian
system, they were later relegated to minor
duties as larger LMS locomotives — such as
'Crab' 2-6-0s and Stanier 'Black Five' 4-6-0s
— were allocated to Scotland. This example
would be withdrawn in 1957. *A. C. J. Ball*

Right:

Tuesday 21 June 1949

Seen in gleaming condition, bearing all the
hallmarks of a well-cared-for locomotive, is
the St Rollox Works shunter, No 56025. Built
in 1890, it was one of 34 locomotives that
once constituted the Caledonian Railway's
'264' class. Shown in plain black, it would
later be repainted in BR's mixed-traffic livery
of lined black and would survive until 1960
— a working life of 70 years. Note on the left
the 'Black Five' 4-6-0, which has just
acquired its new number, 45497. *A. C. J. Ball*

Above:
Tuesday 21 June 1949
Delivered from NBL earlier in the month, Class K1 2-6-0 No 62002 stands in the yard at Eastfield depot in Glasgow, awaiting running-in. Designed by A. H. Peppercorn as mixed-traffic locomotives, the 70 medium-sized 'K1s' served mostly in England, but a number were allocated to Eastfield and Fort William, from where they performed very successfully over the West Highland line. This example would be withdrawn from service in 1966. *A. C. J. Ball*

Below:
Thursday 23 June 1949
Looking very smart with its new British Railways identity, ex-NBR 'Glen' (LNER Class D34) 4-4-0 No 62492 *Glen Garvin* waits at Thornton Junction with an up stopping passenger train. This successful class numbered 32 locomotives, built at Cowlairs Works between 1913 and 1920; this example was outshopped in 1920 and would be withdrawn from service in 1959. *A. C. J. Ball*

Right:

Thursday 23 June 1949
In 1909 W. P. Reid introduced his famous
'Scott' 4-4-0s for use on express passenger
trains. Built in two batches in 1909 and 1911,
all 16 were named after characters from
Sir Walter Scott's 'Waverley' novels.
They were classified 'D29' by the LNER,
which later fitted them with superheaters.
This photograph shows No 62410 *Ivanhoe*
in the busy yard at Dundee. One of the 1911
batch, it would be one of the last to be
withdrawn, in 1952. *A. C. J. Ball*

Below:

Thursday 23 June 1949
At Newburgh, Fife, ex-NBR Class S (LNER Class J37) 0-6-0 No 4598 engages in the kind of work for which it was specifically designed —
hauling a train of coal wagons. Seen in the grimy state typical of goods locomotives during this period, it awaits renumbering. Constructed in 1919
to a W. P. Reid design, it would be withdrawn in 1962. *A. C. J. Ball*

Above:

Friday 24 June 1949

Looking a little the worse for wear, ex-CR Class 294 0-6-0 No 57298 stands on shed at Carstairs. A veteran of 1887, it was built to a Dugald Drummond design introduced in 1883, though its lines are somewhat spoiled here by the addition of a stovepipe chimney.
Still bearing an LMS 28C (Carstairs) shedplate, it would be among the earlier withdrawals of the type, succumbing in 1950. *A. C. J. Ball*

Left:

Friday 24 June 1949

One of a class of 17 locomotives designed by McIntosh, ex-CR Class 652 0-6-0 No 57635 stands quietly at Carstairs depot, showing the sturdy lines of a traditional Caley 0-6-0. Yet to be fitted with its smokebox numberplate, it still bears an LMS 28C (Carstairs) shedplate. Built in 1908, it would remain in service until 1962. *A. C. J. Ball*

Right:

Sunday 7 August 1949

This veteran locomotive bears no clue as to its ownership but has nevertheless had its new number applied. Ex-NBR Class F (LNER Class J88) 0-6-0 tank No 68334 is of the classic 'Dock Tank' design, with a short wheelbase enabling it to negotiate very tight curves. Seen here at Granton in Edinburgh, it is not in steam, as no duties were performed here on Sundays. Built in 1909, it was to put in 50 years' service, eventually being withdrawn in 1959. *E. R. Wethersett*

Below:

Tuesday 9 August 1949

This excellent photograph illustrates the well-balanced lines of the ex-LNER three-cylinder Class V1/V3 2-6-2 tank engine, No 67650 being seen near Dalmeny at the head of an up stopping train to Edinburgh Waverley. Drawn by Nigel Gresley, the 'V1' design was introduced in 1930 with a boiler pressure of 180psi, the 'V3' development, with 200psi boiler, following in 1939. The majority of these versatile locomotives were allocated to depots in Glasgow, Edinburgh, Fife and the North East of England. Built at Doncaster Works in 1936 as a 'V1', No 67650 would be rebuilt as a 'V3' in 1958 and withdrawn from service just three years later, in 1961! *E. R. Wethersett*

Above:
Monday 27 February 1950
Another successful Gresley design, introduced in 1936, was his three-cylinder Class V2 general-purpose 2-6-2. Found all over the LNER system, these locomotives were equally at home on fastgoods services and express passenger trains. With a full head of steam and looking splendid in its new BR livery, No 60969 arrives at Dundee Tay Bridge station with a mixed goods. Built at Darlington Works in 1943, it would serve just 21 years, being withdrawn in 1964. *E. M. Patterson*

Left:
June 1950
Given the amount of water pouring from the overflow, the fireman of ex-LMS Class 5 'Crab' 2-6-0 No 42741 should perhaps be ensuring that the injector is working rather than posing for the photographer. Seen at Beattock Summit with a special train of ICI tank wagons, the locomotive had been built in 1927 at Crewe Works and would be withdrawn in 1965. *P. Ransome-Wallis*

Above:
June 1950
Renumbered by BR but still displaying 'L N E R' on its tender, ex-NBR Class S (LNER Class J37) 0-6-0 No 64558 heads a down goods near Eastfield, Glasgow. Note the full identification on the front buffer-beam — number, class and allocation. Built by NBL in 1918, the locomotive would be withdrawn in 1965. *P. Ransome-Wallis*

Above:
August 1950
Arguably the most versatile general-purpose locomotives used by the LMS were the highly successful Stanier-designed Class 5MT 4-6-0s, known universally as 'Black Fives'. Introduced in 1934, the type was to be found in use all over the LMS system handling all types of traffic, including express passenger services and fast goods trains. No 45159 is seen near Dalcross Junction at the head of an Aviemore–Forres–Inverness stopper; note the veteran bogie coach at the centre of the three-coach train. Built by Armstrong Whitworth in 1935, the locomotive would give 27 years of service before being withdrawn in 1962. *Derek Cross*

2. JANUARY 1951 TO DECEMBER 1956

From the introduction of BR Standard steam locomotives to the eve of the introduction of DMUs and main-line diesel locomotives

The first of BR's new Standard locomotive types appeared in January 1951, when amid much publicity No 70000 *Britannia* was rolled out of Crewe Works. The Standard classes began to arrive in Scotland in the summer of 1951, when five Class 5MT 4-6-0s were allocated to Perth depot. Class 6MT 'Clan' Pacifics arrived at Polmadie depot in Glasgow early in 1952, Class 4MT 2-6-4 tanks being delivered to Polmadie, Corkerhill and Kittybrewster depots throughout the same year. Early in 1953 a handful of Class 4MT 2-6-0s were delivered to Motherwell and Stirling depots, but it was not until 1954 that increasing numbers of these Standard locomotives were delivered to depots in Scotland. During 1955 larger numbers of '4MT' 2-6-4 tanks were delivered to Polmadie, Corkerhill, Kittybrewster, Keith, Dundee and Perth depots, examples of '5MT' 4-6-0s being delivered to Polmadie, Eastfield, Corkerhill, Perth and St Rollox, also during 1955 and 1956.

The increasing number of new locomotives allowed for the disposal of many older locomotives and sometimes complete classes. During the early 1950s almost the entire remaining stock of ex-Highland Railway and Great North of Scotland Railway locomotives were shipped off for scrap, while virtually all the ex-North British Railway 4-4-0 classes disappeared from the stock book, only a very few examples surviving until the late 1950s.

Towards the end of 1948 the Railway Executive had formed a committee to compare the relative merits of steam, diesel and electric motive power. This committee did not report until 1951, in the meantime a working party was formed to evaluate the use of lightweight diesel trains. The conclusion of the investigation was outlined in yet another report in March 1952, which led to the introduction of these lightweight diesel trains, known as diesel multiple-units (DMUs).

In December 1954 the British Transport Commission published its plan for the 'Modernisation and Re-equipment of British Railways'. In locomotive terms this predicted the end of steam power by announcing that no new steam locomotives would be built after the end of the 1956 programme. A Pilot Scheme was devised whereby 174 main-line diesel locomotives would be purchased, from various manufacturers, and subjected to rigorous testing before further orders were placed. In all 160 of these locomotives would be built with electric transmission, and these would range from an 800hp Type A (later Type 1) for goods work to a 2,300hp Type C (4) for express passenger trains. In practice orders were placed for large numbers of locomotives without any prolonged testing, with the result that some designs with inherent problems were produced and consequently had very short lives.

While work on building diesel locomotives was progressing, steam ruled supreme. For example, Stanier 'Black Fives', based in large numbers at both Inverness and Perth, worked virtually all the traffic between those two centres, as well as to/from Wick/Thurso and Kyle of Lochalsh. They were assisted by a few ex-Caledonian Class 3P 4-4-0s and some newly arrived Standard Class 5MT 4-6-0s based at Perth. Suburban traffic around Edinburgh was in the hands of Gresley Class V1 and V3 tanks, and coal traffic originating from the pits in Fife was in the capable charge of a large number of ex-NBR Class B and S (LNER Class J37) 0-6-0s, ex-LNER Class J38 0-6-0s and Austerity Class 8F 2-8-0s based at the Fife depots, with Thornton Junction at their centre.

Left:
Saturday 16 June 1951
Designed specifically for use on the West Highland line from Glasgow to Fort William and Mallaig, the Class K4 three-cylinder 2-6-0 locomotives proved a great success and continued to work on this route until steam traction was replaced by diesel power in 1960/1. This photograph shows No 61995 *Cameron of Locheil* working the 4.50pm Fort William–Mallaig service near Banavie. Although bearing its British Railways number, it remains in green livery and still sports the letters 'L N E R' on the tender. One of this class managed to survive into preservation: No 61994 *The Great Marquess* was bought privately and was due to undergo a major overhaul during 2005/6. *E. D. Bruton*

Right:

Saturday 23 June 1951
With a full head of steam and displaying its new British Railways identity, ex-LMS Class 5MT 4-6-0 No 44959, a Perth locomotive, looks in fine fettle as it heads a down train of oil tanks through Stirling station. Built at Horwich Works in 1946, it would be withdrawn in 1965. *E. D. Bruton*

Below:

Saturday 11 August 1951
Also stalwarts on the West Highland line were the 'K2' Moguls. Introduced to the line by the LNER after the Grouping, they remained predominant until supplemented in the 1950s by Peppercorn Class K1 Moguls and Stanier 'Black Five' 4-6-0s. Here No 61782 *Loch Eil* departs Fort William with the 11am goods to Mallaig. Built by Kitson & Co in 1921, this locomotive would be withdrawn from service in 1960. *Ian S. Pearsall*

Above:
Monday 20 August 1951
Proudly bearing its new British Railways identity, ex-CR Class 300 0-6-0 No 57655 moves slowly through the yard at Carstairs depot. The '300s' were the last class of 0-6-0 tender locomotive to be built by the Caledonian Railway; designed by William Pickersgill and constructed between 1918 and 1920, most survived to work for the new British Railways. This example, built in 1919, would remain in service until 1962. *Ian Allan Library*

Below:
September 1951
Probably one of the most ungainly-looking classes of locomotive, the ex-LMS Class 5MT 'Crab' 2-6-0s were nevertheless reliable and popular with crews. No 42793, built at Crewe Works in 1927 and destined to be withdrawn in 1964, is seen near Thankerton with a down goods.
Ian Allan Library

Above:

Tuesday 17 June 1952

A reminder of the powerful ex-Caledonian 4-6-0 classes of locomotive, Class 60 No 54650 is seen near Uddingston with a train of empty wagons including steel- and wooden-bodied vehicles. Designed by William Pickersgill and introduced in 1916, the class originally consisted of only six locomotives, but surprisingly the LMS built a further 20 examples during the 1920s. In their early years these powerful superheated locomotives were utilised on express passenger trains, until superseded by the newer LMS classes of the 1930s. No 54650 was one of the original batch built in 1916 and would survive until 1953. *E. R. Wethersett*

Right:

Thursday 19 June 1952

Seen here in the spectacular setting of the Forth Bridge, ex-LNER Class D11/2 4-4-0 No 62675 *Colonel Gardiner* heads an up stopping train. The 'D11/2' sub-class was built specifically to the North British Railway's loading-gauge, and a large number were allocated to Eastfield depot in Glasgow and Haymarket depot in Edinburgh. This locomotive, built by Kitson & Co in 1924, would be one of the early withdrawals, in 1959. *E. R. Wethersett*

Above:
Tuesday 22 July 1952
One of the first of its type to be delivered, in July 1951, Standard Class 5MT 4-6-0 No 73007 was allocated to Perth depot and is seen here leaving Perth with the 'Granite City' for Aberdeen. About a year old when photographed, it looks still to be in fine condition. Built at Derby Works, it was to serve 15 years, being withdrawn in 1966. Note the number of goods wagons in the yard behind the train; also the lower-quadrant signals, which would remain in use until replaced by colour lights in the early 1960s.
R. K. Evans

Left:
Wednesday 23 July 1952
Seen here in the slightly less spectacular setting of the Tay Bridge is ex-NBR Class L (LNER Class C16) 4-4-2 tank No 67499 working an up stopping train. This well-balanced design of locomotive was the superheated version of the earlier 'C15' tank. Built in 1921 by NBL, No 67499 would be one of the earlier class withdrawals, in 1955.
E. R. Wethersett

Above:

July 1952

Another of the powerful ex-CR Class 60 4-6-0 locomotives still in use in the early 1950s was No 54640. One of the LMS batch built in 1926, it is seen in grimy condition near Balornock, working a train of empty coaching stock. By now among the last of the type in service, it would be withdrawn later in 1952. *C. Lawson-Kerr, Ian Allan Library*

Right:

April 1953

Built at Crewe Works the previous year and allocated to Polmadie in Glasgow, BR Standard Class 6MT 'Clan' Pacific No 72002 *Clan Campbell* makes a fine sight climbing Beattock with a Birmingham–Glasgow express. Only 10 'Clans' were built; originally intended for use on the ex-Highland main line to Inverness, they were instead allocated to Polmadie and Kingmoor and used on the West Coast main line. This locomotive would be withdrawn after only 10 years' service, in 1962. *P. Ransome-Wallis*

Above:

April 1953
The double-heading of heavy passenger trains was common practice on the West Coast main line. This Edinburgh/Glasgow–Manchester express is in the charge of two of Stanier's classic locomotive designs. Seen near Nethercleugh, north of Lockerbie, Class 5MT 4-6-0 No 44670, a Polmadie-allocated locomotive, is piloting ex-LMS Class 6P 'Jubilee' 4-6-0 No 45728 *Defiance*, and both are working hard with the load. The 'Black Five', built at Horwich Works as late as 1950, would survive just 16 years before being withdrawn in 1966. The 'Jubilee' was built at Crewe in 1936 and would be withdrawn in 1962. *P. Ransome-Wallis*

Below left:
Saturday 6 June 1953
On a bright summer's day ex-NBR Class F (LNER Class J88) 0-6-0 tank No 68345 shunts a short goods train at Alloa. Introduced in 1904 to a design by W. P. Reid, these tall-funnelled, short-wheelbase, dumb-buffered locomotives were used primarily for shunting dock and harbour lines. Some survived until the early 1960s; this example, built in 1912, would be withdrawn 50 years later, in 1962. *J. L. Stevenson*

Right:
Saturday 6 June 1953
Working a Strathaven–Scotstoun excursion, ex-CR Class 60 4-6-0 No 54639 is seen near Rutherglen. Built by the LMS in 1926, it would be the last of the class to be withdrawn, later in 1953. *K. K. MacKay*

Above:
Wednesday 24 June 1953
Ex-CR Class 113 4-4-0 No 54466 pauses in the beautiful surroundings of Moy station with the 3.22pm Aviemore–Inverness train. Designed by William Pickersgill and introduced in 1916, these graceful-looking superheated locomotives were classified '3P' by the LMS and BR. This example, built at St Rollox Works in 1916, is in excellent external condition — a credit to the staff at Aviemore depot, who obviously took a pride in their work. Still at Aviemore, it would be withdrawn from service in 1962. *R. F. Roberts*

Above:

Wednesday 24 June 1953

In the 1940s and '50s the 'Black Five' 4-6-0s could be found hauling passenger and goods trains throughout the ex-Highland Railway system and formed the hard-working core of the motive power on these lines. Seen working a lengthy southbound goods at Ballinluig, on the Highland main line between Inverness and Perth, is No 45483. Built for the LMS at Derby Works in 1943, it would survive until 1966. *R. F. Roberts*

Below:

Saturday 1 August 1953

The crew of ex-LNER Class V3 2-6-2 tank No 67672 monitor their progress as they enter Dunfermline Lower station at the head of a stopping service for Edinburgh Waverley. The 'V1s' and 'V3s' were to be seen working the intensive suburban services around Edinburgh until replaced by DMUs in 1958 — and around Glasgow until replaced by the electric 'Blue Train' EMUs introduced in 1960/1. This locomotive had been built at Doncaster in 1938 as a 'V1' and was rebuilt as a 'V3' in 1943; it would be withdrawn from service in 1962. *Brian Morrison*

Above:

August 1953

The graceful lines of this locomotive are a clue to its Great North of Scotland Railway origin. Looking well cared-for by the staff at Keith depot, ex-GNSR Class T (LNER Class D41) 4-4-0 No 62241 waits at Craigellachie with a Boat of Garten service (via the Speyside line). The design was introduced in 1895 by William Pickersgill, this example being built in the same year by Neilson & Co. A few of these fine locomotives lingered in service until finally withdrawn in the early 1950s, this example succumbing later in 1953. *P. B. Whitehouse*

Above:

August 1953

Looking handsome with its proper chimney (instead of the stovepipe variety fitted to some of the class), the station pilot at Carstairs stands resplendent in ex-works condition after an overhaul. One of 10 locomotives built for the LMS in 1925 to the Caledonian Railway's '439' design, Class 2P 0-4-4 tank No 55261 would be withdrawn in 1961. One of the earlier Caledonian-built examples survives in preservation, No 55189 of 1908 now being in the care of the SPRS at Bo'ness. *D. T. Greenwood*

Above:
Tuesday 27 April 1954
Ex-LMS Class 5MT 4-6-0 No 44981, allocated to Kentish Town shed in North London, leaves Hurlford for Carlisle with a test train consisting of a dynamometer car, two mobile test vehicles and a bogie van, while the tender appears to have come from a 'Princess Royal' or 'Princess Coronation' Pacific. Built at Crewe Works in 1946, the locomotive would be withdrawn from service in 1967. *Ian Allan Library*

Below:
Sunday 27 June 1954
Sir William Stanier's 'Princess Coronation' Pacifics of the 1930s and '40s were the mainstay of Anglo-Scottish express passenger trains on the West Coast main line until the advent of the English Electric Type 4 diesels in 1958. Seen approaching Beattock Summit with an up express is No 46222 *Queen Mary*, a Polmadie-allocated locomotive. Built in 1937 as one of the streamlined examples of the class (the casing having been removed in 1946), it would remain in service until 1963. *John Robertson*

Above:
Tuesday 29 June 1954
Featuring one of the 'A3' Pacifics that were the mainstay of express passenger services on the East Coast main line, this excellent photograph shows No 60057 *Ormonde* storming up the North Queensferry gradient prior to crossing the Forth Bridge with the 12.40pm Aberdeen–Edinburgh Waverley. One of several of the class allocated to Haymarket depot in Edinburgh, this locomotive had been built at Doncaster Works in 1925 and would be withdrawn in 1963. *E. D. Bruton*

Right:
Wednesday 8 September 1954
From their introduction in the late 1930s until supplemented in the 1950s by Standard Class 5s the 'Black Five' 4-6-0s provided the motive power for the bulk of operations on the ex-Highland main line, No 45460 being seen hard at work near Pitlochry with the 8.20am Inverness–Perth. Built at Crewe Works in 1938, it would be withdrawn from service in 1965. *R. J. Morris*

Above:
Saturday 19 March 1955
Scotland had its fair share of the ex-LMS Fowler/Stanier/Fairburn Class 4MT 2-6-4 tanks, most allocated to Glasgow and Ayrshire depots.
A Fairburn version built at Derby Works in 1946 and based at Polmadie, No 42245 is seen at Carluke with a Glasgow Central–Lanark service.
Note the Caledonian-style route indicator, which was still being used by local crews; this one shows a correct 'Main Line via Motherwell' route.
The locomotive would be withdrawn in 1964. *Ian S. Pearsall*

Left:
Sunday 17 April 1955
Suitably painted in black lined livery, handsome ex-NBR Class D (LNER Class J83) 0-6-0 tank No 68474 was one of the Edinburgh Waverley pilots. Allocated to St Margarets depot, it was kept immaculately clean by the staff and in this view even has white smokebox embellishments. Built by Sharp, Stewart & Co in 1901, it would be among the earlier class withdrawals, in 1958.
Ian Allan Library

Above:
Saturday 7 May 1955
Ex-NBR 'Superheated Scott' (LNER Class D30) 4-4-0 No 62434 *Kettledrummle* leaves Dundee Tay Bridge station with a train for Tayport, on the south bank of the River Tay. Still in good condition, this locomotive had been built in 1915 and would be withdrawn from service in 1958.
John Robertson

Right:
Saturday 28 May 1955
Freshly outshopped from Cowlairs Works after an overhaul, ex-GNR Class H3 (LNER Class K2) 2-6-0 No 61746 stands in the yard at Eastfield depot in Glasgow. This particular locomotive bears a 40A (Lincoln) shedplate, but after the Grouping about 20 of the class were allocated to Scottish depots, the Eastfield examples spending most of their time on the West Highland line. Built at Doncaster in 1916, No 61746 would be withdrawn in 1959.
W. A. C. Smith

Above:
Wednesday 29 June 1955
Built by the Highland Railway (at its Lochgorm Works in 1905) specifically for light branch work, 0-4-4 tank No 55051 ended its days working on the Dornoch branch and is seen here shunting in the yard at The Mound, junction for the branch. It would be withdrawn in 1956, replaced by an 0-6-0 pannier tank transferred from the Western Region. *R. F. Roberts*

Below:
Saturday 16 July 1955
Allocated to Kittybrewster depot in Aberdeen, ex-GNR Class H3 (LNER Class K2) 2-6-0 No 61783 *Loch Sheil* leaves Keith Junction with a Keith–Aberdeen train. Built by Kitson & Co in 1921, it would be withdrawn in 1959. *L. Marshall*

Right:
Saturday 30 July 1955
Ex-LNER Class D49/1 'Shire' 4-4-0
No 62713 *Aberdeenshire*. Slowing for the
stop at Kinghorn with a Thornton Junction–
Edinburgh Waverley stopping train. The
'Shires', introduced in 1927, were used
primarily on services between Edinburgh,
Glasgow, Dundee and Perth. By 1955
18 locomotives, the majority named after
Scottish counties, were allocated to depots at
Thornton Junction, Dundee, Stirling and
Edinburgh, while two further Scottish Region
examples were actually based in England, at
Carlisle Canal depot, for use on the Waverley
route. Built at Darlington Works in 1928,
No 62713 was allocated to Thornton Junction,
whence it would be withdrawn in 1957. Sister
locomotive No 62712 *Morayshire*, purchased
privately for preservation, can now be found
in the care of the SRPS at Bo'ness.
Adam Arnott

Above:
Wednesday 17 August 1955
Although barely a year old, Standard Class 3MT 2-6-0 No 77015, seen near Busby Junction with the 8pm Glasgow St Enoch–Kilmarnock service,
looks less than well cared-for externally. Built at Swindon Works, it was one of a batch delivered to Scotland (allocated to Hurlford depot) in the
summer of 1954 and would be withdrawn in 1966 after only 12 years in service. The Caledonian-style route indicators were introduced to the ex-
GSWR lines from St Enoch by the LMS after the Grouping. *Ian S. Pearsall*

Above:
Wednesday 17 August 1955
Accelerating past Busby Junction with a Glasgow (College)–Kilmarnock goods train, veteran ex-CR '812' 0-6-0 No 57589 looks in fine fettle, given its 55 years in harness. Built in 1900 to a McIntosh design, it would be withdrawn in 1956. Fortunately another of this class has been saved for posterity: No 57566 can be found on the Strathspey Railway at Aviemore. *Ian S. Pearsall*

Below:
Wednesday 17 August 1955
In LMS days about 70 Class 2P 4-4-0s were transferred to Scottish depots, mostly around Glasgow and Ayrshire, and after Nationalisation some examples found their way to Kittybrewster depot in Aberdeen. Here we see Hurlford resident No 40592 near Pollokshaws with the 7.10pm Glasgow St Enoch–Kilmarnock service. Built by the LMS at Derby Works in 1928, this locomotive would be withdrawn from service in 1961. Again, the Caledonian-style route indicator confirms a Kilmarnock service. *Ian S. Pearsall*

Above:
Monday 5 September 1955
The Gresley-designed three-cylinder Class V1 and V3 2-6-2 tanks became the prime motive power for the Edinburgh suburban services during later LNER days and remained thus until displaced by DMUs in 1958. On a fine summer's day we see 'V1' No 67666 working an 'Inner Circle' train between Craiglochart and Morningside Road stations. Built at Doncaster Works in 1938, this locomotive would be rebuilt as a 'V3' as late as 1961 — a year before withdrawal! *W. S. Sellar*

Right:
Thursday 15 September 1955
BR Standard Class 5MT 4-6-0 No 73063 was built at Derby Works and delivered in September 1954 to Polmadie depot in Glasgow, where it is seen still in good condition a year later. It was to serve just 12 years in total, being withdrawn in 1966. *Philip J. Kelley*

Above:
Saturday 17 September 1955
During 1954 and 1955 a number of new Standard Class 4MT 2-6-4 tanks were allocated to Kittybrewster depot in Aberdeen. Here we see
No 80122, barely a month old, departing Keith Junction with a stopping train for Aberdeen. Built at Brighton Works, this locomotive would be
withdrawn just 11 years later, in 1966. *John Robertson*

Below:
Tuesday 20 September 1955
Ex-CR '812' 0-6-0 No 57597 leaves Keith Junction with a goods for Elgin via the Highland line. Built in 1900, this veteran locomotive, allocated to
Inverness, would be withdrawn from service in 1962. *P. H. Wells*

Above:
Friday 23 September 1955
Coupled to a single coach, BR Standard Class 4MT 2-6-4 tank No 80121 waits at the bay platform at Keith Junction. Another Brighton-built locomotive, new to Kittybrewster depot in the summer of 1955, it would be withdrawn in 1966. *P. H. Wells*

Below:
Sunday 22 April 1956
Seen near Croy on the NBR route between Edinburgh and Glasgow, ex-LNER Class A4 Pacific No 60009 *Union of South Africa* heads a local mixed train to Glasgow Queen Street. Looking in excellent condition, it was based at Haymarket depot in Edinburgh for most of its working life, finally being transferred to Aberdeen Ferryhill to work the fast three-hour express services between Aberdeen and Glasgow. Built at Doncaster in 1937 as LNER No 4488, it would be withdrawn in 1966 and sold to a private buyer. It has since hauled many specials throughout the UK and is currently based on the Severn Valley Railway. *Ian S. Pearsall*

Above:
Sunday 10 June 1956
Barely two years old but already looking uncared-for, BR Standard Class 7MT 'Britannia' Pacific No 70052 *Firth of Tay* stands on shed at its home depot of Polmadie in Glasgow. Built at Crewe Works in August 1954 as one of the last batch of this class, it would be withdrawn less than 13 years later, in April 1967. *David A. Anderson*

Below:
Friday 22 June 1956
On a fine summer's day Class B1 4-6-0 No 61358, a St Margarets locomotive, arrives at Tynehead station with the 4.10pm stopping train from Edinburgh Waverley to Hawick. One speculates whether the group of children on the platform are prospective passengers or simply waiting 'to see the train'. Built at Darlington in 1949, the locomotive would be withdrawn barely 14 years later, in 1963. *T. G. Hepburn / Rail Archive Stephenson*

Above:
Friday 22 June 1956
Ex-LNER Class K1/1 2-6-0 No 61997 *MacCailin Mor* leaves Lochailort with the 4.50pm train from Fort William to Mallaig. This unique locomotive was a Thompson two-cylinder rebuild (in 1945) of a Gresley Class K4 and was the precursor to the Peppercorn 'K1s' built in 1949/50. Having spent most of its working life on the West Highland line, it would be withdrawn in 1961. *R. F. Roberts*

Right:
Sunday 26 August 1956
Seen near Annan on the ex-GSWR main line, ex-LMS Class 5MT 4-6-0 No 45362 heads for Dumfries with a down goods. Built by Armstrong Whitworth in 1937, this locomotive would be withdrawn in 1962 after 25 years of service. *R. Leslie*

3. JANUARY 1957 TO DECEMBER 1967

From the introduction of DMUs and main-line diesel locomotives to the end of main-line steam

January 1957 saw the introduction of diesel multiple-units (DMUs) on the intensive Edinburgh Waverley–Glasgow Queen Street services, these being Swindon-built, six-car 'Inter-City' trains. Quickly deemed a great success, they were followed in 1958 by two-car DMUs on suburban services around Edinburgh. Main-line diesel locomotives started to appear in Scotland in 1959 in the shape of 27 BRCW/Sulzer Type 2s, allocated initially to Inverness, Kittybrewster (Aberdeen) and Dundee. They were followed by seven English Electric Type 1s, shared between Kittybrewster and Inverness, and 19 BR/Sulzer Type 2s, all based at Inverness. All three classes proved a great success, and it was not long before further, more powerful classes followed them into service in Scotland; by the summer of 1961 diesel locomotives had displaced steam traction from all lines north of Perth and Aberdeen. During the same period diesel locomotives replaced steam on services between Glasgow, Fort William and Mallaig, and similarly between Glasgow and Oban via Stirling. Meanwhile, deliveries of new Standard steam locomotives culminated in the arrival in 1957 of 10 Class 5MT 4-6-0s

fitted with Caprotti valvegear at St Rollox depot in Glasgow and of 25 Class 4MT 2-6-0s at depots throughout Scotland.

The result of all this activity was that large numbers of steam locomotives could be seen stored out of use awaiting movement to the scrapyards. The vast majority were pre-Grouping types, ex-CR and ex-NBR veteran 0-6-0 tender and tank locomotives. As the delivery of reliable diesel locomotives increased, growing numbers of post-Grouping locomotives were also being scrapped. Class V1 and V3 tanks disappeared almost overnight from Edinburgh when the suburban services were 'dieselised', and by the early 1960s increasing numbers of 'B1s', 'V2s' and Pacifics had also vanished to join the queues at scrapyards. One highlight of this period was the transfer in 1962 to Ferryhill and St Rollox depots of a number of 'A4' Pacifics to operate a new fast timetable of services between Aberdeen and Glasgow. This they did until 1966, when the last five survivors at Aberdeen were withdrawn.

As more diesels arrived, the remaining steam locomotives were concentrated in areas where they could best be utilised and effectively run down before scrapping.

One most prominent area was the Ayrshire coalfield, where large quantities of coal were being transported to Ayr harbour for shipment to power stations in Northern Ireland. The mainstay of these operations were veteran Caley 0-6-0s and ex-LMS 2-6-0 'Crab' locomotives allocated to Ayr depot. But the inevitable happened, and in October 1966 all steam locomotives were withdrawn from this traffic, to be replaced by diesel power.

Mention must be made of the most exciting change to the scene around Glasgow in 1960, with the introduction of the electric 'Blue Trains'. Early in November the new service was introduced between Airdrie and Helensburgh through Glasgow Queen Street Low Level and proved an immediate success with the public. Unfortunately technical problems brought about its withdrawal six weeks later, and steam-hauled coaching stock continued to run for a further 10 months before the electric service could be reinstated in October 1961. A number of the original electric multiple-units would continue to operate the service until late 2002, giving more than 40 years of service.

The allocation of main-line steam in Scotland ended in June 1967, when the final two locomotives were withdrawn from service. The last survivors, shunting colliery sidings in Fife, were ex-NBR Class J36 0-6-0s Nos 65288 and 65345, built in 1897 and 1900 respectively, and it is a great credit to their designer that they remained hard-working to the end.

Left:
Saturday 20 April 1957
Demonstrating that the staff at Keith depot took pride in their new locomotives, BR Standard Class 4MT 2-6-4 tank No 80122, not quite two years old, looks in fine fettle as it prepares for its next duty at Elgin. Built at Brighton Works in 1955, it would serve just 11 years, being withdrawn in 1966.
A. A. Cameron

Right:
Monday 22 April 1957
Impressed with the 0-6-0 diesel-electric shunters introduced in 1944 by the LMS, British Railways continued their construction from 1953. This example, still bearing its pre-1957 number (13215) at St Rollox depot, was built at Derby Works in 1956. Renumbered D3215 and again in the 1970s as 08 147, it would eventually be withdrawn in 1983.
R. E. Vincent

Above:
Monday 22 April 1957
In 1953 the North British Locomotive Co (NBL) in Glasgow introduced an 0-4-0 diesel-hydraulic shunting design for British Railways.
This example, seen still bearing its pre-1957 number (11705) at South Leith in Edinburgh, was built in 1955. Eventually renumbered D2705,
it would be withdrawn in 1967. *R. E. Vincent*

Left:
Tuesday 23 April 1957
Built in 1895, ex-CR Class 19 0-4-4 tank No 55124 was a true veteran by the time it was photographed shunting at Dumfries station. Finally withdrawn in 1961 after a working life of 66 years, it would be stored for a while at Dalry Road depot in Edinburgh before finally being removed to the scrapyard. *R. E. Vincent*

Below:
Friday 2 August 1957
One of the batch of CR '812' 0-6-0s built in 1899, No 57554 is seen — somewhat surprisingly — in charge of a Rutherglen–Balloch Central passenger train leaving Partick West station. Apparently in extremely poor condition, it would nevertheless manage a further three years before withdrawal. *G. H. Robin*

Left:
Tuesday 27 August 1957
In charge of a heavy goods train, ex-LNER Class K3 2-6-0 No 61986 heads south through Strathbungo station. Built at Darlington in 1937, this locomotive would be withdrawn in 1962. *G. H. Robin*

Above:

Monday 2 September 1957

Introduced in 1900, the 0-4-4 tank engines of the CR's '439' class numbered 78 examples, all of which lasted into BR days. Prior to their replacement by DMUs they could be found on branch-line duties in and around Edinburgh, No 55214 being seen at Grangemouth station at the head of a train for Larbert. Built in 1912, this locomotive would be withdrawn in 1961. *P. H. Groom*

Above:

Saturday 19 October 1957

Apparently in need of some maintenance, ex-GNSR Class F (LNER Class D40) 4-4-0 No 62277 *Gordon Highlander* departs Craigellachie with the 3pm Elgin–Keith goods. Built by NBL in 1920 to a design by Thomas Heywood, this locomotive would be withdrawn in 1958 but following refurbishment and repainting would be used on special workings throughout 1959/60 before being placed in the Glasgow Transport Museum. *G. C. Holyhead*

Above:
Saturday 19 April 1958
Introduced on Edinburgh Waverley–Glasgow Queen Street passenger services in January 1957, the Swindon-built, six-car 'Inter-City' DMUs found immediate favour with the travelling public. Seen here at Lenzie on the 12.0 Edinburgh–Glasgow service is just such a set, with car Sc79111 leading. *Ian S. Pearsall*

Below:
Saturday 19 April 1958
Photographed from the same spot, ex-NBR Class C (LNER Class J36) 0-6-0 No 65228, an Eastfield-allocated locomotive, passes Lenzie with an unfitted ballast train. Built in 1891, this veteran would soldier on until in 1962, giving a total of 71 years' service. *Ian S. Pearsall*

Above:
Saturday 3 May 1958
Ex-CR '812' 0-6-0 No 57579 works an up goods train near Kilmuir. New in 1900, this locomotive would be withdrawn a year earlier than No 65228, featured in the previous picture, having given 61 years of service. *Ian S. Pearsall*

Below:
Saturday 12 July 1958
Passenger traffic over the Waverley route may have been light, but large amounts of goods traffic traversed the line between Carlisle and Edinburgh. The ex-LNER Class V2 2-6-2s were regular performers, No 60965 being seen at Hawick with a northbound goods. Built at Darlington Works in 1943, this St Margarets-based locomotive would be withdrawn only 19 years later, in 1962. *K. L. Cook*

Above:
Friday 29 August 1958
In late-summer sunshine ex-LMS Class 5MT 4-6-0 No 45476 pauses at Achnasheen with the 6.20am mixed train from Kyle of Lochalsh to Inverness. This Inverness-based locomotive had been built at Derby Works in 1943 yet would be withdrawn only 21 years later, in 1964. *N. Caplan*

Below:
Wednesday 26 November 1958
One of the early successes among the Pilot Scheme diesels was the BRCW/Sulzer Type 2. Seen stabled behind the signalbox at Duddingston & Craigmillar station in Edinburgh is No D5303, built in 1958. Renumbered 26 003 under the TOPS scheme, it would remain in service until 1993. *Iain Smith*

Above:
Saturday 28 March 1959
BR Standard Class 5MT 4-6-0 No 73055 calls at Troon station
with an Ayr–Glasgow express. Built at Derby Works in 1954,
this Polmadie-allocated locomotive would be withdrawn after
only 12 years' service, in 1966. *G. H. Robin*

Below:
Saturday 23 May 1959
Barely a month before withdrawal, ex-LNER Class D49/1 4-4-0
No 62715 *Roxburghshire* leaves Gorebridge station with the
Saturdays-only 12.0 Hawick–Edinburgh Waverley train. Built in
1928 at Darlington Works, this locomotive spent most its life
based at St Margarets depot in Edinburgh. *W. S. Sellar*

Above:
Tuesday 14 July 1959
Photographed during the month of its withdrawal, ex-LMS Class 2P 4-4-0 No 40688, built at Crewe in 1932, calls at Glengarnock station with a train from Glasgow St Enoch to Kilmarnock via Dalry. *G. H. Robin*

Below:
Tuesday 14 July 1959
Class 5MT 4-6-0 No 44669, a Carlisle Kingmoor locomotive, climbs out of Girvan with the 2.10pm Glasgow St Enoch–Stranraer boat train.
Built by British Railways at Horwich Works in 1949, it would be withdrawn just 18 years later, in 1967. *Eric W. H. Greig*

Above:
Wednesday 29 July 1959
The Caledonian Railway's '300' class represented the last 0-6-0 tender locomotives designed for that company. No 57667, seen working a Ballachulish–Oban goods at Appin station, was built in 1918 and would be withdrawn in 1962. *K. R. Pirt*

Above:
July 1959
With express headcode already in place, Class K1 2-6-0 No 62012, built by NBL in 1949, stands on the turntable at Mallaig prior to working a train to Fort William. This locomotive would be one of the last of its type in service, surviving until 1967. *K. R. Pirt*

Above:
July 1959
A pair of ex-NBR Class M (LNER Class C15) 4-4-2 tanks were retained until early 1960 to work the Craigendoran–Arrochar push-pull trains. Here No 67474, built in 1913 by the Yorkshire Engine Co, is held at Craigendoran Lower while ex-LMS Class 5MT 4-6-0 No 44998 heads an excursion from Craigendoran Pier to Glasgow. The 'C15' would be withdrawn in 1960, while the 'Black Five', built at Horwich Works in 1947, would remain in service until 1967. *P. Ransome-Wallis*

Above:
Tuesday 18 August 1959
Ex-LMS Class 5MT 4-6-0 No 44954 approaches Kirkcaldy station with the 6.58am Leuchars–Glasgow Queen Street working. Another Horwich locomotive, this 'Black Five', built in 1946, would serve 20 years, being withdrawn in 1966. *Ian Allan Library*

Above:
September 1959
A scene at Dingwall which epitomises operations north of Inverness just prior to the introduction of diesel traction. The passenger train from Inverness to Kyle of Lochalsh leaves behind ex-LMS Class 5MT 4-6-0 No 44997, piloted by ex-CR Class 72 4-4-0 No 54487, which will be detached at Achanalt. No 54487 had been built for the Caledonian by Armstrong Whitworth & Co in 1921 and would be withdrawn from service in 1961; the 'Black Five', dating from 1947, was yet another Horwich-built example destined to serve just 20 years — half the working life of its companion here.
S. C. Crook

Right:
Friday 11 September 1959
This detailed study of ex-LMS Class 2P 4-4-0 No 40574 shows its to be in good external condition, albeit a shade dusty! Built at Derby Works in 1928, it had been allocated to Hurlford and Ayr depots for most of its working life and would survive a further couple of years before being withdrawal in 1961. *G. W. Morrison*

Above:
April 1960
Ex-GNR Class H3 (LNER Class K2) 2-6-0 No 61784 climbs through
Glenfinnan with a train of empty fish vans heading for Mallaig. This
was one of the few un-named 'K2s' to be allocated to Scottish depots.
Built by Kitson & Co in 1921, it would survive a further year, being
withdrawn in 1961. *S. C. Crook*

Below:
Friday 20 May 1960
With McCaig's Tower prominent in the background, this location
could only be Oban. Drawing a train of empty coaching stock out of
the station is ex-CR Class 439 0-4-4T No 55238. This locomotive,
one of the last to be built for the Caledonian, in 1922, would be
withdrawn in 1961. *M. Mensing*

Right:
Monday 20 June 1960
One of the most momentous changes to the railway scene in Glasgow was the introduction in November 1960 of the 'Blue Train' suburban electric services between Airdrie and Helensburgh. Prior to this date much rebuilding of stations was carried out, and driver-training with the new stock.
This photograph shows a new three-car EMU at Milngavie station on one such driver-training turn. *R. F. Roberts*

Below:
Saturday 6 August 1960
A pair of Class 5MT 4-6-0s — ex-LMS No 45036 leading BR Standard No 73100 — at Maybole station with a Stranraer Harbour–Glasgow St Enoch boat train. The 'Black Five' was an early example, built at the Vulcan Foundry in 1934, and would be withdrawn from service in 1962; No 73100, a lifelong Corkerhill locomotive, was built at Doncaster in 1955 and would be withdrawn in 1967. *G. H. Robin*

Above:
Saturday 27 August 1960
Bearing a Perth shedplate, ex-CR '72' 4-4-0 No 54486 calls at Pitlochry station with a Blair Atholl–Perth local. Some of these local services had already been turned over to DMUs (in 1959), so it is surprising that this locomotive, built in 1920, was to survive a further two years before withdrawal. *S. Summerson*

Below:
Monday 5 September 1960
Seen working hard as it leaves Crianlarich Upper with a goods train from Fort William to Glasgow is ex-LMS Class 5MT 4-6-0 No 44975. A Crewe Works example built in 1946 and by now allocated to Stirling depot, it would be withdrawn in 1965. *J. C. Haydon*

Right:
Thursday 15 September 1960
On a fine sunny day ex-LMS Class 4MT 2-6-4 tank No 42272, a Dalry Road locomotive, departs Stirling station with the 10.15am to Edinburgh Princes Street. One of the Fairburn variants, this locomotive, built at Derby in 1947, would serve just 15 years, being withdrawn in 1962. *D. J. Lane*

Below:
Sunday 9 October 1960
Working hard at the rear of the 10am Glasgow Queen Street–Kirkcaldy train, ex-NBR Class A (LNER Class N15/2) 0-6-2 tank No 69131 will bank the train up the gradient to Cowlairs, where it will slip the coupling before working back to Queen Street. Built by NBL in 1910, this locomotive would remain in service until 1962. *S. Rickard*

Above:
Saturday 4 February 1961
Amidst evidence of a recent snowfall, ex-LNER Class V2 2-6-2 No 60834 heads a Hawick–Carlisle stopper near Longtown. Built at Darlington Works in 1938, it would survive a further three years before being withdrawn, in 1964. *R. Leslie*

Above:
Saturday 15 April 1961
Ex-LNER Class V2 2-6-2 No 60958 climbs out of Whitrope Tunnel with an Edinburgh–Carlisle goods. The 'V2s' were regular performers on the Waverley route, more than 25 being allocated to St Margarets depot in Edinburgh at this time. One of the later-built locomotives, turned out by Darlington Works in 1942, this example would last another 20 months before withdrawal. *R. Leslie*

Right:

Saturday 13 May 1961

A more detailed view of a 'V2' as No 60873
Coldstreamer, another St Margarets
locomotive and the only named Scottish
example, takes water at Hawick station.
Built at Doncaster in 1939, it would be
among the earlier class withdrawals, in 1962.
Ian Allan Library

Below:

Monday 22 May 1961

The 10 BR Standard Class 6MT 'Clan'
Pacifics spent much of their time on the
West Coast main line, working expresses and
stopping trains. The first five were allocated
to Glasgow's Polmadie depot, the remainder
to Carlisle Kingmoor. Seen here at its home
depot is one of the former, No 72003
Clan Fraser, turned out by Crewe Works
early in 1952. All five Polmadie examples
would be withdrawn late in 1962 — after
barely 10 years' service — and stored at
that depot until sent for scrap in 1964.
J. C. Haydon

Above:
Friday 26 May 1961
With the impressive structure of Ayr station in the background, ex-LMS Class 5MT 'Crab' 2-6-0 No 42917 drifts through with a coal train.
Built at Crewe in 1930, it would give a total of 36 years' service before withdrawal in 1966. *D. Butterfield*

Below:
June 1961
In excellent external condition, ex-LNER Class V3 2-6-2 tank No 67616 heads a two-coach passenger train near Ardrossan Town station.
Built at Doncaster Works in 1931 as a 'V1', it was rebuilt as a 'V3' in 1960 only to be withdrawn in 1962. *E. M. Patterson*

Above:
July 1961
Ex-LNER Class B1 4-6-0 No 61178 passes Whitrope Siding signalbox with a southbound goods. This was another type common on the Waverley route, more than 15 examples being allocated to St Margarets depot at this time. This locomotive was built by the Vulcan Foundry in 1947 and would be withdrawn from service in 1964. *D. E. Esau*

Right:
July 1961
Seen at Dunfermline depot is NBL-built 0-4-0 diesel-hydraulic shunter No 11718; although built in 1957 it carries a 'pre-1957' number. Eventually renumbered D2718, it would be withdrawn in 1967, after only 10 years' service. *David C. Smith*

Above:

Wednesday 9 August 1961

Arguably the most successful of the Pilot Scheme diesel designs was the English Electric Type 1. Seven early examples, fitted with token-exchange apparatus for single-line working, were allocated to Kittybrewster in Aberdeen, the first being No D8028, seen at Aviemore depot. Built by Robert Stephenson & Hawthorn in 1959, this locomotive would be renumbered 20 028 under the TOPS scheme and withdrawn in 1992. *J. Hunt*

Above:

Thursday 31 August 1961

Veteran ex-NBR Class F (LNER Class J88) 0-6-0 tank No 68335 shunts the sidings at Gorgie Mills in Edinburgh. Built in 1909, this locomotive, one of the last survivors of its class, would be withdrawn from service in 1962. *The Rev R. T. Hughes*

Above:

Friday 1 September 1961

Many suburban services around Edinburgh were turned over to DMU operation from 1958, when two-car units built by the Gloucester Railway Carriage & Wagon Co were delivered. One such unit is seen arriving at Polmont station on the 1.55pm service from Falkirk Grahamston. *S. Rickard*

Above:

Friday 23 February 1962

In a scene epitomising southwest Scotland in the early 1960s ex-CR '812' 0-6-0 No 57572 waits in the southbound loop at Auchinleck while ex-LMS Class 5MT 'Crab' 2-6-0 No 42834 storms past with a southbound goods. No 57572 was built in 1899 and would be withdrawn in 1963 after 64 years' service; the 'Crab', built at Horwich Works in 1930, would give 'only' 32 years of service before withdrawal in 1962. *Derek Cross*

Above:
Saturday 21 April 1962
Allocated to Corkerhill depot in Glasgow, BR Standard Class 4MT 2-6-4 tank No 80045 works a Glasgow St Enoch–Largs train just south of Largs.
Note the continued use of the Caledonian-style route indicator. Built at Brighton Works in 1952, the locomotive would be withdrawn from service
in 1967. *S. Rickard*

Above:
Saturday 28 April 1962
Two days prior to the official closure of the line, a Gloucester RCW two-car DMU pauses at East Pilton station, on the Edinburgh Princes Street–
Leith North branch. The station had been opened in 1934 to serve the large engineering works of Bruce Peebles & Co, visible behind the train.
G. M. Staddon/ N. E. Stead collection

Above:
Thursday 10 May 1962
Seen at Carstairs, ex-CR '439' 0-4-4 tank No 55189 attaches through coaches from Edinburgh to the rear of the morning Glasgow–Liverpool express. Note the impressive signal gantry at the northern end of the station. Built in 1908, the apparently careworn locomotive managed to survive into preservation following withdrawal in 1962 and can now be seen at work on the Bo'ness & Kinneil Railway. During restoration the stovepipe chimney seen here was replaced by the correct Caledonian-style version. *Derek Cross*

Above:
Saturday 19 May 1962
Visiting from Carlisle, BR Standard Class 7MT 'Britannia' Pacific No 70018 *Flying Dutchman* stands on shed at Polmadie, Glasgow. Built at Crewe Works in 1951, it would be withdrawn in 1966. *David C. Smith*

Above:
Saturday 26 May 1962
Another successful class of diesel locomotive, introduced in 1959 as part of the Pilot Scheme, was the BR/Sulzer Type 4 'Peak', built at Derby Works. The initial 10 were followed in the years 1960-2 by 183 more powerful locomotives, construction of which was shared between Derby and Crewe. Seen here leaving St Boswells station with an Edinburgh Waverley–Carlisle stopper is No D13, built at Derby in 1960 and here displaying a 55H (Leeds Neville Hill) shedplate. Renumbered 45 001 under the TOPS scheme, it would be withdrawn in 1986. *M. Mensing*

Left:
May 1962
During 1961 British Railways started to take delivery of the most powerful of its early main-line diesel locomotives, the English Electric-built Type 5 'Deltics'. Twenty-two of these had been ordered to replace steam traction on the East Coast main line, of which eight were allocated to Haymarket depot in Edinburgh. This excellent photograph shows No D9018 *Ballymoss* emerging from Calton Tunnel at the head of the up 'Talisman'. Built at the Vulcan Foundry in 1961, it would be withdrawn just 20 years later. *Eric Treacy*

Above:
Thursday 21 June 1962
Glasgow's 'Blue Train' services were
launched to great public acclaim in November
1960 only to be withdrawn six weeks later due
to serious technical problems, but following
its reintroduction 10 months later in October
1961 the intensive service became highly
successful. Here one of the three-car EMUs —
built locally at the Pressed Steel works at
Linwood — prepares to leave Springburn with
a service to Milngavie. The last survivors of
the original units were to continue in operation
until 2002. *S. Creer*

Right:
Monday 9 July 1962
In 1957 BR(W) '16xx' 0-6-0 pannier tanks
Nos 1646 and 1649 were sent north to
Helmsdale depot as replacements for the pair
of ex-HR 0-4-4 tanks that had worked the
Dornoch branch. Seen after closure of the
branch (in 1960), No 1649 performs station-
pilot duties at Dingwall. Built at Swindon
Works in 1951, it would continue in service
for a further five months. *Author*

Left:
Sunday 26 August 1962
Looking unusually unkempt for a Corkerhill-based locomotive, BR Standard Class 4MT 2-6-0 No 76095 stands on shed between turns at its home depot. Built in 1957 at Horwich Works, it would be withdrawn early in 1967 after less than 10 years' service. *A. J. Wheeler*

Above:
Tuesday 2 October 1962
In disgraceful condition, its identity barely discernible, ex-NBR Class C (LNER Class J36) 0-6-0 No 65288 works the morning goods from Queensferry to Edinburgh. This veteran of 1897 was destined to be one of Scotland's final pair of BR steam locomotives to be withdrawn, in June 1967, after 70 years of service. *The Rev R. T. Hughes*

Above:
Friday 30 November 1962
One of the successful Swindon-built six-car
'Inter-City' DMUs, car Sc79096 leading, waits
to leave Edinburgh Waverley on a service to
Glasgow Queen Street. *M. Mensing*

Right:
Friday 22 February 1963
Built in 1892 to a design introduced by
Dugald Drummond in 1883, ex-CR '294'
0-6-0 No 57360 is seen in an awful state at
Motherwell depot. Having been reinstated
following the failure of the newly delivered
Clayton Type 1 diesels, it would finally be
withdrawn the month after this photograph
was taken, having given more than 70 years
of service. The *Rev R. T. Hughes*

Above:
Wednesday 2 October 1963
Bearing an Ardrossan shedplate, ex-LMS Class 5MT 'Crab' 2-6-0 No 42806 passes Polmadie with a lengthy goods. Built at Crewe Works in 1928, it would be withdrawn in 1963. *M. Bryce*

Left:
Friday 4 October 1963
Class B1 4-6-0 No 61344 passes Saughton Junction, Edinburgh, with a special goods train consisting largely of brake vans. One of only 10 examples of the class to be built at Gorton Works, in 1949, the locomotive was to remain in service until 1966.
The Rev R. T. Hughes

Right:
Saturday 21 March 1964
Class A1 Pacific No 60152 *Holyrood* was a regular performer over the Waverley route between Edinburgh and Carlisle, but here we see it preparing to leave Waverley station with a local train for Berwick-upon-Tweed. Designed by the LNER's last CME, A. H. Peppercorn, and built at Darlington Works in 1949, it would serve only 16 years before withdrawal in 1965. Unfortunately none of this class survived into preservation, but a new locomotive, No 60163 *Tornado*, is currently being constructed at Darlington by the A1 Steam Locomotive Trust. *Author*

Above:

Saturday 28 March 1964
Filling the skies with an unholy mix of
smoke and steam, ex-LMS Class 5MT 4-6-0
No 45176, assisted at the rear by an ex-LMS
Class 4MT 2-6-4 tank, storms Beattock with
a northbound coal train. An early example,
built by Armstrong Whitworth in 1935,
the 'Black Five' was to remain in service
until 1966. *J. S. Whiteley*

Left:

Tuesday 31 March 1964
A fine shot of a 'Black Five' working hard as
No 44980 climbs to Gleneagles, on the ex-CR
main line between Perth and Stirling, with
an up goods. One of the later examples, built
at Crewe in 1946, the locomotive would be
withdrawn after a career of less than 20 years,
in 1965. *Paul Riley*

Above right:

Saturday 25 April 1964
Resting between duties at Edinburgh Waverley goods depot is Clayton Type 1 No D8568. This unique centre-cab design was introduced in 1962
and was a versatile but short-lived class of locomotive. With two Paxman engines, power could be fed to one, two or four traction motors depending
on the load being hauled, and these diesels were regularly to be seen in pairs hauling heavy goods trains on the difficult Waverley route.
Despite their unreliability they seemed to perform well on this work, but all would be withdrawn by 1971. Sold into industrial use, No D8568 would
eventually pass into preservation, becoming the sole surviving example, and can currently be found on the Chinnor & Princes Risborough Railway.
The *Rev J. D. Benson*

Left:
Saturday 9 May 1964
Ex-LNER Class A3 Pacific No 60042
Singapore approaches Falahill Summit, on the
Waverley route, with an Edinburgh–Carlisle
goods. Built at Doncaster Works in 1934, it was
by now just two months from withdrawal, in
July 1964. *Ian Allan Library*

Below left:
Wednesday 27 May 1964
Having arrived from Whithorn, BR Standard
Class 2MT 2-6-0 No 78026 shunts its goods
train into the yard at Newton Stewart. Goods
services on the Whithorn branch would survive
a further five months, complete closure being
effected in October 1964. The locomotive was
to fare little better; built at Darlington Works in
1954, it would be withdrawn in 1966. *J.
Spencer Gilks*

Right:
Tuesday 2 June 1964
The gracefully sleek lines of Gresley's
masterpiece are clearly evident as ex-LNER
Class A4 Pacific No 60004 *William Whitelaw*
simmers quietly at St Margarets depot in
Edinburgh. Built at Doncaster Works in 1937 as
No 4462, it was originally named *Great Snipe*
and was later renamed after the LNER's first
Chairman. One of the last examples of its class,
it would survive until 1966. *Author*

Below:
Thursday 11 June 1964
Two days prior to the withdrawal of the service,
BR Standard Class 2MT 2-6-0 No 78048
arrives at St Boswells with the 6.35pm from
Berwick-upon-Tweed via the Tweed Valley line.
The locomotive, built at Darlington Works in
1955, was also doomed, being withdrawn the
following month after less than nine years'
service. *David C. Smith*

Left:
Sunday 28 June 1964
Criticised for their unreliability, the Clayton Type 1s were good workhorses nonetheless and could be seen working goods trains in pairs throughout southern Scotland. However, Nos D8514 and D8502, seen near Greskine, still require the services of a banker as they climb Beattock Bank with a northbound goods. No D8514, leading, was built in 1963 and would be withdrawn in 1968 after only five years' service; D8502, new in 1962, would last slightly longer, until 1971. *Derek Cross*

Below:
Tuesday 30 June 1964
This splendid photograph shows BR Standard Class 5MT 4-6-0 No 73153 working hard with a Glasgow–Dundee express near Dunblane. This locomotive was one of the batch built at Derby Works in 1957 and fitted with Caprotti valve gear in an attempt to improve efficiency of maintenance. Allocated to St Rollox depot in Glasgow, it was to last only nine years, being withdrawn in 1966. *A. R. Thompson*

Right:

Wednesday 22 July 1964
BR Standard Class 7MT 'Britannia' Pacific
No 70007 *Coeur-de-Lion,* allocated to
Carlisle Kingmoor shed, approaches
Dunblane with a Crewe–Perth express.
Built at Crewe Works in 1951, it would
be withdrawn in 1965. *Paul Riley*

Below:

Thursday 23 July 1964
In another splendid photograph showing a
'Black Five' hard at work, No 44722 storms
out of Perth station with the late-running
7.10am Aberdeen–Glasgow express. This
locomotive was one of the later examples of
the class, built at Crewe in 1949, and would
thus manage just 18 years' service before
withdrawal in 1967. *Paul Riley*

Above:
Saturday 25 July 1964
Class 4MT 2-6-4 tank No 42125 darkens
the skies over Beattock while banking a
northbound goods at Greskine. One of the
Fairburn variants, this locomotive was built
at Derby Works in 1949 and would be
withdrawn in 1966. *Derek Cross*

Left:
Sunday 26 July 1964
The BR Standard version of the LMS Class
4MT 2-6-4 tank numbered 155 locomotives,
built at Brighton, Derby and Doncaster
over a period of six years from 1951 to 1957.
Allocated to depots as far apart as
Kittybrewster (Aberdeen) and Brighton,
they were very capable workhorses and
soon became popular with crews. No 80007,
built at Derby Works in 1952, was allocated
originally to Polmadie, Glasgow, but is seen at
St Margarets, Edinburgh, complete with 64A
shedplate. Withdrawal would come in 1966.
N. E. Preedy

Above:

Wednesday 5 August 1964
The NBL Type 2 diesels, the first of which were ordered as part of the Pilot Scheme, quickly came to be regarded as 'lame ducks', and all were transferred to Scottish depots, so as to be closer to the manufacturer for repairs! However, based primarily at Eastfield in Glasgow or Kittybrewster in Aberdeen, they managed to find suitable duties throughout Scotland; until replaced by BRCW Type 2s they worked services from Glasgow to Oban and to Dundee, and the Buchan branches and Elgin services from Kittybrewster. No D6141 is seen leaving Banchory with the daily goods train for Aberdeen. Built in 1960, it would be withdrawn after only seven years. *P. H. Wells*

Right:

Saturday 8 August 1964
BR Standard Class 6MT 'Clan' Pacific No 72009 *Clan Stewart* approaches Gleneagles with the 9.25am Crewe–Aberdeen express. The last of the 'Clans' to be built, in 1952, this locomotive was one of five allocated to Carlisle Kingmoor depot and would also be one of the last to be withdrawn, in 1965. Although none of the class was to escape the cutter's torch, the Standard Steam Locomotive Co, based on the Swanage Railway in Dorset, plans to construct a new 'Clan', No 72010 *Hengist. A. W. Martin*

Left:
Saturday 24 April 1965
Following overhaul at Inverurie Works
ex-LMS Class 5MT 4-6-0 No 44998 spent
a few days 'running in' at Ferryhill depot in
Aberdeen before returning to its home shed
of Perth. It is seen here in ex-works condition,
preparing to leave Aberdeen station with
a train of empty coaching stock. Built at
Horwich Works in 1947, it would survive
a further two years, being withdrawn in
April 1967. *Author*

Below:
Saturday 24 April 1965
BR Standard Class 4MT 2-6-4 tank No 80117
prepares to depart Dalbeattie with the 2.50pm
service from Dumfries to Kirkcudbright. The
Kirkcudbright branch was to close two weeks
after this photograph was taken, the main line
— the 'Port Road' between Dumfries and
Stranraer — following suit within two months.
Built at Brighton Works in 1955, No 80117
would itself survive for less than a year.
David C. Smith

Above:
April 1965
A common sight during the mid-1960s was of steam and diesel traction working side by side. At the foot of Calton Tunnel in Edinburgh, Brush Type 4 No D1577 approaches Waverley station with a football special from London. This class would be one of the most successful of the 1960s designs, more than 500 examples being constructed; No D1577, built in 1964 (and renumbered 47 457 under TOPS), would survive until 1992. In the background, awaiting the 'road' with a train of empty coaching stock, is BR Standard Class 4MT 2-6-4 tank No 80022. One of the earliest examples built (at Brighton Works in 1951), it would be withdrawn only two months later, in June 1965, having given only 14 years' service. *W. J. V. Anderson*

Right:
Saturday 29 May 1965
On a damp and dismal day ex-LNER Class A3 Pacific No 60052 *Prince Palatine*, looking in fine fettle, is prepared for a special working from Waverley station. By this time it was one of only two 'A3s' still in BR service (the other being No 60041 *Salmon Trout*), No 60103 *Flying Scotsman* having been sold to a private buyer in 1963. Built at Doncaster Works in 1924, it would survive another eight months, eventually being withdrawn as the last of its class in January 1966. *Author*

Above:

Tuesday 6 July 1965

With the Ochil Hills in the background, ex-WD Class 8F 2-8-0 No 90515 drifts eastbound, near Bogside, Fife, with a train of rails. Designed by R. A. Riddles for the Ministry of Supply, more than 900 examples of this class were built between 1943 and 1945 by Vulcan Foundry and by NBL in Glasgow. After D-Day many worked overseas in mainland Europe, being returned to the UK following the end of hostilities. This locomotive, built by Vulcan Foundry in 1945 and numbered 79251 by the War Department, was to end its days based at Dunfermline depot, where it would be withdrawn only four months after this photograph was taken. *Gerald T. Robinson*

Left:

Saturday 28 August 1965

Another success among the Pilot Scheme diesel designs was the English Electric Type 4, introduced from 1958 and eventually numbering 200 locomotives. Here No D359 passes through Edinburgh's Princes Street Gardens, approaching Waverley station with an Aberdeen–Edinburgh express. Built at Vulcan Foundry in 1961, it would be withdrawn in 1982 as No 40 159. *Brian Stephenson*

Above:
August 1965
Following the withdrawal of goods services in June 1965 the Ballachulish branch would remain open to passenger traffic for only a further seven months. Here BRCW/Sulzer Type 2 No D5367 enters Benderloch station with an evening train from Oban. New in 1962, the locomotive would be withdrawn in June 1985 as No 27 021. *Andrew Muckley*

Below:
August 1965
A Cravens two-car DMU awaits to depart Banchory station with a service from Aberdeen to Ballater. The 'Royal Deeside line' would close to passenger traffic soon afterwards, in February 1966. *Andrew Muckley*

Left:
August 1965
In an attempt to reduce costs and increase
revenue on sparsely populated lines British
Railways introduced railbuses on several
routes in Scotland. One of the longest, at 51
miles, was that from Aviemore to Elgin via
Craigellachie. It included five request stops,
one of which — Gilbey's Cottages Halt —
is seen playing host to a Park Royal railbus.
Andrew Muckley

Above:
August 1965
NBL-built Type 2 No D6123 calls at Dyce station with a Fraserburgh–Aberdeen train. In an attempt to improve its reliability this locomotive
was re-engined in June 1963 with a more powerful Paxman unit in place of its MAN original. After extensive testing the experiment was judged
a success, and a further 19 locomotives of the class were similarly equipped. New in 1959, No D6123 would be withdrawn in 1971,
while the passenger service on the Fraserburgh branch would last only until October 1965. *Andrew Muckley*

Above:
Friday 10 September 1965
BR/Sulzer Type 2 No D5120 passes Alyth Junction, on the ex-Caledonian main line between Perth and Aberdeen, with an up goods train. Bearing an Inverness shedplate, the locomotive is also fitted with miniature snowploughs, as well as a tablet-catcher for single-line working. BR's own Type 2 design was among the more successful of the early diesels, and this example, built at Derby Works in 1960, would survive to be renumbered 24 120 under the TOPS scheme before being withdrawn in 1976. *R. F. Roberts*

Right:
Sunday 12 September 1965
By the mid-1960s the clean lines of Glasgow's 'Blue Train' EMUs had been disfigured by the addition of yellow warning panels. This photograph, taken at Bridgeton Central, shows unit No 021 waiting to depart on the 4.5pm service to Clydebank. The leading car is No Sc75586.
R. F. Roberts

Left:
Thursday 28 April 1966
One of just eight locomotives now remaining of a class of 168, ex-NBR Class C (LNER Class J36) 0-6-0 No 65319 shunts a rake of coal wagons at Lower Bathgate prior to working them into Bathgate yard. Built in 1899, this veteran would be withdrawn from service barely six months after the photograph was taken. *David C. Smith*

Below left:
Tuesday 3 May 1966
Waiting to leave Perth station at the head of the 7pm train to Aberdeen is ex-LMS Class 5MT 4-6-0 No 45461. Built at Crewe Works in 1938 and by now allocated to Perth depot, it would be withdrawn in August 1966. *Verdun Wake*

Right:
Tuesday 10 May 1966
One of the early NBL 0-4-0 diesel-hydraulic shunters, built in 1955 as No 11704, No D2704 stands on shed at Dunfermline. It would be withdrawn in 1967. *P. Foster*

Above:
Friday 17 June 1966
Ex-LNER Class A4 Pacific No 60019 *Bittern* leaves Perth station with the 09.50 Perth–Aberdeen. Built in 1937 at Doncaster Works, *Bittern* was by now one of the last five 'A4s' in service and following withdrawal in September 1966 would be bought privately for preservation. It would go on to operate many main-line enthusiast specials and is currently undergoing a major rebuild at Ropley, on the Mid-Hants Railway. *R. E. B. Siviter*

Above:

Wednesday 29 June 1966

Built in 1960 by Robert Stephenson & Hawthorn, English Electric Type 1 No D8031 passes Carron station at the head of a pick-up goods from Craigellachie to Aviemore. Renumbered 20 031 under the TOPS scheme, this locomotive would be withdrawn by BR in October 1989 and is now preserved on the Keighley & Worth Valley Railway in Yorkshire. *John M. Boyes*

Below:

Thursday 23 March 1967

By 1967 the only BR steam locomotives still working in Scotland were a pair of ex-NBR Class C (LNER Class J36) 0-6-0s, one of which, No 65345, is seen shunting a rake of coal wagons at Seafield Colliery, near Kirkcaldy, Fife. Built in 1900, it would finally be withdrawn in June, having given 67 years of service; classmate No 65288, built in 1897, would be withdrawn in the same month, after 70 years of service. *Derek Cross*